Palm Springs Paradise

Vintage Photographs from America's Desert Playground

Peter Moruzzi

Gibbs Smith
TO ENRICH & INSPIRE HUMANKIND

Dedicated to the Palm Springs Historical Society for its resolute stewardship of the desert's photographic legacy.

First Edition
25   11

Text © 2015 Peter Moruzzi

Published by
Gibbs Smith
P.O. Box 667
Layton, Utah 84041

1.800.835.4993 orders
www.gibbs-smith.com

Designed by Kurt Wahlner
Printed and bound in China

Gibbs Smith books are printed on either recycled, 100% post-consumer waste, FSC-certified papers or on paper produced from sustainable PEFC-certified forest/controlled wood source. Learn more at www.pefc.org.

Library of Congress Cataloging-in-Publication Data

Moruzzi, Peter.
  Palm Springs paradise : vintage photographs from America's desert playground / Peter Moruzzi. — First edition.
     pages cm
  ISBN 978-1-4236-3991-6
1. Palm Springs (Calif.)—History—Pictorial works. 2. Palm Springs (Calif.)—Social life and customs—Pictorial works. 3. Historic buildings—California—Palm Springs—Pictorial works. 4. Architecture—California—Palm Springs—History—Pictorial works. 5. Palm Springs (Calif.)—Buildings, structures, etc.—Pictorial works. I. Title..
  F869.P18M53 2015
  979.4'97—dc23
                    2015000620

Image Credits

All images are from the collection of the Palm Springs Historical Society, except those noted below.

Pages 1, 77 (large), 109 (right): Courtesy of Tayva Martinez.

Pages 3, 6, 47 (both), 67, 68, 71, 72–73 (right), 74–75 (right), 76, 77 (inset), 79, 81, 82, 83 (both), 87 (bottom), 88, 88–89 (right), 90 (left), 90–91 (right), 92, 93, 94–95 (right), 96–97 (right), 104–05 (right), 115 (right), 116–17 (all), 118 (right), 119 (both), 121 (right), 122 (right), 123, 124–25 (left), 127 (right), 138, 139 (right), 142, 146, 148 (left, top), 152–53 (right): Photographs by Paul Pospesil.

Page 8: Courtesy of Seaver Center for Western History Research, Natural History Museum of Los Angeles County.

Pages 8–9 (right), 33 (background), 41 (background, top): Photograph by Paul Pospesil and Earl Cordrey.

Pages 14–15 (right): Photograph by Mission Art Company.

Pages 16–17 (center), 17 (right, top): Photographs by W. W. Lockwood.

Pages 26 (left, bottom), 28–29 (right), 30, 114–15 (left), 125 (right, top & bottom), 126–27 (left), 128 (background), 131 (bottom), 135 (right & inset), 136–37 (all), 148 (right), 156–57 (right), endsheet 6: Photographs by Winfield Line.

Pages 28–29 (right): Photograph by Noel W. Frederick II.

Page 36 (inset & background): Photograph by Anthony Burke.

Page 38: Courtesy of Wide World Photos.

Page 42: Photograph by Dick Whittington.

Pages 45 (right), 50 (top), 78 (left), 141 (right), 156 (left, top): Gayle's Studio Collection, courtesy of Tracy Conrad and Paul Marut. Photographs by Gail B. Thompson.

Pages 48, 58–59 (right), 66 (top), 70, 84, 85, 87 (top), 120 (all), 120–21 (background), 122 (left; background), 143, 144 (right), 160 (inset), 161 (both), 164, 169, 172 (both), 173, 174: Photographs by George Aquino.

Pages 48–49 (right), 65, 69, 106, 112, 134–35 (left): Courtesy of the Palm Springs Art Museum. Photographs by Bill Anderson.

Pages 52, 72, 86 (top), 102–03 (left), 107, 108, 109 (left), 110–11 (left), 128–29 (right), 144 (left), 145, 147, 149, 150–51 (left), 160 (large), endsheet 4, back cover: Courtesy of Charles Phoenix.

Page 54: Photograph by Edward Canby.

Page 60: Courtesy of Western Resort Publications. Photograph by Ferris H. Scott.

Page 80: Photograph by Ames Color Press.

Page 100 (left): Gayle's Studio Collection, courtesy of Tracy Conrad and Paul Marut. Photograph by Frasher's Inc.

Page 100 (right): Photograph by Orville Logan Snider Photography.

Page 103: Photograph by Jack Albin.

Page 104: Photograph by American Airlines News Bureau.

Page 128 (bottom): Courtesy of KDES/RR Broadcasting.

Page 131 (right, top): Photograph by William Scarlott.

Page 133: Photograph by *Palm Springs Life*.

Page 151 (right): Photograph by UPI.

Page 154 (right, top): Photograph by Mike Roberts.

Page 155 (right): Photograph by Waltah Clarke's Photo Shop.

Page 156 (left, bottom): Photograph by Roberts Royal.

Pages 159, 163, endsheet 2: Courtesy of the Palm Springs Art Museum.

Page 165: Courtesy of the John F. Kennedy Presidential Library and Museum, Boston, Massachusetts. Photograph by Robert Knudsen.

Pages 166–67 (right), 168 (left, top; right): Photographs by Fred Weigel.

Pages 176: Photograph by James Schnepf.

Contents

City National Bank is ready for its close-up.

Introduction

Since *Palm Springs Holiday* was published a few years ago, interest in the city's fascinating and glamorous past has continued to grow. Upon hearing that the venerable Palm Springs Historical Society had recently digitized one hundred years of photographs—over thirty thousand in total—I knew a book was waiting amidst that treasure trove. And I was right. Over many days I systematically viewed every image, narrowing the archive down to two hundred of the most compelling, outrageous, surprising, and fun. Some might be familiar; most will be unknown. So join me for another journey through time, from Palm Springs' earliest days as an isolated outpost through its transformation into America's foremost desert resort.

FACING: Head over heels at the Palm Springs Tennis Club. RIGHT: When a lone palm on North Indian Avenue was worth naming a hotel after.

Early Palm Springs

Palm Springs is the ancestral home of the Agua Caliente Band of Cahuilla Indians, who lived in the Coachella Valley for centuries before white people began colonizing the area to grow crops in the late nineteenth century. Floods and drought quashed that experiment.

The area was next promoted as a tubercular sanatorium, but that was not to be Palm Springs' destiny. Through toil and grit, the early pioneers—mostly sturdy women—forged a Shangri-la out of a failed agricultural colony and middling hospice. The transformation of Palm Springs into a winter playground was astonishingly rapid. By 1925, automobiles from Los Angeles—and the transcontinental railroad from the Midwest and East—filled the village with tourists. Palm Springs also attracted its share of artists, photographers, and sun-baked eccentrics, who chose the desert for inspiration.

Palm Springs, c. 1887, when it was known as Palm Valley and still part of San Diego County. The low desert was to be an agricultural paradise as well as a sanatorium for sufferers of lung disease. Unfortunately, the Southern California real estate bust and several years of drought put an end to this early land boom in the Coachella Valley.

LEFT: Serious men, serious mules, c. 1900, when Palm Springs was an Old West frontier town. RIGHT, TOP: Pedro Chino in the doorway of his home in 1898. Wife Marie, on the left, weaves a large basket. RIGHT, BOTTOM: Lavinia Crocker's Tent Homes for Invalids, c. 1899. Dr. Harry and Nellie Coffman would buy Mrs. Crocker's property in 1910, initially operating it as the Desert Inn Hotel and Sanatorium.

Mrs. Crocker's Tent Homes for Invalids
Palm Springs   Riverside Co. Cal.

Street Scene, Palm Springs, Cal.

140 - PALM SPRINGS, CAL.

LEFT, TOP: Palm Canyon Drive, when trees vastly outnumbered people. LEFT, BOTTOM: Taking a stroll in downtown Palm Springs, c. 1915. At Palm Springs Stage and Store, gasoline was dispensed from metal barrels with spigots. In the middle is Bunker's Garage, operated by local dynamo Zaddie Bunker. FACING: The Agua Caliente Band's original bathhouse.

116 - Agua Caliente Bath House, Palm Springs, Cal.

13

ABOVE: Of sturdy river rock construction, Otto Adler's La Palma Hotel on Palm Canyon Drive boasted "We Never Sleep." Hopefully, that wasn't true of his guests. RIGHT: The hotel's dining room displayed a map showing the two routes to Palm Springs from Los Angeles by miles. The La Palma Hotel, depicted as an oasis at the foot of Mount San Jacinto, was at mile 110.

20-Hotel La Palma
Palm Springs, Cal.

ABOVE: Dr. Harry Coffman was the Desert Inn Hotel and Sanatorium's resident physician until he left wife Nellie in 1914 for a new life in the Imperial Valley. RIGHT: Picnicking in Andreas Canyon in 1912. FACING, TOP: A horse-drawn excursion. FACING, BOTTOM: Desert Inn tent cabin in 1911. "23 skidoo" meant "to leave quickly," which Mrs. Browning and daughter Ruth seem disinclined to do.

PALM SPRINGS, CAL.

THE DESERT INN GUESTS IN ANDREAS PALM SPRINGS, CAL. FE

-1912- PHOTO BY W.W. LOCKWOOD

THE DESERT INN,
PALM SPRINGS, CAL.   ALL ABOARD FOR ANDREAS CANY

The Skidoo
23
23

The new Palm Springs Hotel, c. 1925. RIGHT: Rules and regulations for Welwood Murray's original Palm Springs Hotel, c. 1910. Note "that any expectoration, whether in rooms or grounds, be exclusively made in paper napkins, to be carefully consumed by fire."

Palm Springs Hotel

BOARD:
- $2.00 TO $2.50 PER DAY.
- $10.00 TO $14.00 PER WEEK.

SPECIAL MONTHLY RATES.

BREAKFAST FROM 7 TO 8.   LUNCH FROM 12 TO 1.
DINNER FROM 5:30 TO 6:30.

Laws Regulating the Liability of Hotel Keepers.

SECTION 1 of the law relating to the liability of hotel keepers reads as follows: "Whenever the proprietor of any hotel shall post in a conspicuous manner in the room occupied by any guest, a notice requiring such guest to bolt the door, or, on leaving, to lock the door and leave the keys at the office, and to deposit his money, jewels and ornaments in the office safe, and if such guest neglects to do so, the proprietor of such hotel shall not be liable for anything which may be lost or stolen from said room."

Rules and Regulations.

1. Guests will please register their names upon arrival.
2. Proprietors will not be responsible for valuables unless left in office safe. Extra charge will be made for meals or refreshments served in rooms. Make application at office for extras or any requirements. No deduction will be made for missed meals. Parties occupying rooms will be charged for board unless by other agreement.
3. All bills are payable weekly. Guests will not be given the benefit of monthly rates unless contract is made in advance, nor of weekly and monthly rates if they remain less than the week, or month, as agreed upon.
4. No washing, ironing or cooking will be permitted in the rooms.
5. Laundry work done for guests. Give list of all articles to chambermaid, to be returned to office.
6. No chairs or any furniture to be taken from the rooms.
7. To prevent danger to all concerned from fire, do not read or smoke while in bed. No light whatever to be left burning when absent from rooms.
   Guests will please report any neglect of the help.
9. Fires in rooms charged extra. Leave orders for fuel at office.
10. SPECIAL.—For sanitary and precautionary reasons, and for general comfort, the proprietors consider it incumbent upon them to exact as essential and obligatory, that any expectoration, whether in rooms or grounds, be exclusively made in paper napkins, to be carefully consumed by fire. These can be procured at office. Any guest having troublesome cough will please avoid as much as possible any annoyance thereby to others.

Mineral Hot Baths, 35 cents each, or three tickets for $1.00. Stage fare from R. R. Station and return, $1.50. Trunks and Baggage, extra. Telephone charges as usual. Conveyances to the Palm and other cañons may be had on application.

Detecting the likeness of Abraham Lincoln on mountainsides was common in the early twentieth century. Here, Abe's profile appears above the village as he gazes skyward. It can still be seen today from the corner of Palm Canyon Drive and Amado Road.

ABOVE: Palm Springs pioneers Zaddie Bunker, daughter Frances, and husband, Ed, in 1914. Mechanic Zaddie would manage Bunker's Garage after Ed left to run a ranch in Garner Valley. BELOW: Moving Tilly's Chicken Shack restaurant to Cathedral City. RIGHT: "Nature boy" William Pester at his Palm Canyon cabin, c. 1920.

Scottish painter Gordon Coutts's Moroccan villa on South Patencio Road in 1924. Today it's the Korakia Pensione.

Dashing horseman Frank Bogert in the 1930s. Among his occupations was publicity man for the El Mirador, manager of the Racquet Club, cofounder of Thunderbird Dude Ranch, rodeo announcer, and four-term mayor of Palm Springs. He died in 2009 at age 99.

The Thirties and Forties

*I*n the 1930s, Palm Springs visitors thumbed their noses at the Depression and continued to arrive in steady numbers. New hotels arose to accommodate them. On the periphery, illegal gambling thrived. And like a mirage in the hot and windy desert, the fabulous Racquet Club materialized out of sand and scrub in the north end of Palm Springs. Irwin Schuman's Chi Chi, which opened under that name in 1936, would morph into a space-age nirvana twenty years later.

Palm Springs was incorporated in 1938. In early 1942, after America entered World War II, the Coachella Valley became a training site for desert tank combat under the command of General George Patton. Palm Springs' El Mirador Hotel was transformed into Torney General Hospital for the war's duration. Following the war, residential and commercial construction exploded in Palm Springs. Celebrities, industrialists, and the average Joe chose Palm Springs as their winter destination.

RIGHT: Irwin Schuman's Chi Chi in 1946. FAR RIGHT: Hmmm, Indio or Palm Springs?

LEFT: The infamous Dunes Club in Cathedral City, where, from 1931 until 1943, it hosted illegal gambling in elegant style. BELOW: Palm Springs High School on Ramon Road. RIGHT: The new pool at Deep Well Guest Ranch, set amongst the tumbleweeds. Today, it's the Deepwell Estates neighborhood of Palm Springs.

ABOVE: The stately air-conditioned Royal Palms Hotel in 1946. RIGHT: Cruising past the Chi Chi is General Petroleum's entry in the Desert Circus Parade.

BELOW: Pearl McManus's famous Palm Springs Tennis Club before its 1946 modernist expansion. The oval pool with its two palms became a worldwide symbol of Palm Springs.
RIGHT: The Hotel del Tahquitz in 1945. It sits where Santa Fe Federal Savings & Loan—now the Palm Springs Art Museum Architecture and Design Center—would be built in 1961.

LEFT: Movie stars Charlie Farrell and Ralph Bellamy opened their Racquet Club in 1936. Although located in the desolate north end of Palm Springs, it attracted Hollywood's top celebrities and moguls. ABOVE: The exclusive Smoke Tree Ranch colony was founded in the 1930s as a winter escape for the well-to-do. Horseback riding was—and remains—integral to its appeal.

The Fabulous El Mirador

Appearing as a Spanish Colonial outpost in the desert, the El Mirador was the brainchild of Prescott T. Stevens. He bet big on the El Mirador, borrowing a large pot of money to build a first-rate, full-service resort at the edge of town. Upon its completion in 1928, the El Mirador met all expectations, boasting an Olympic-size swimming pool and the first golf course in the Coachella Valley. Unfortunately, the stock market crash and ensuing economic meltdown crushed Stevens financially. He lost the property to creditors in 1931 and died the following year.

Under the dynamic new leadership of Warren Pinney, the El Mirador hired a young Frank Bogert in the mid-1930s as its publicity man to escort and photograph its famous guests. During his eighty years in the desert, Bogert—unpretentious, robust, self-invented—palled around with industrialists, celebrities, presidents, and royalty. He later became the city's cowboy mayor, the personification of Palm Springs. A bronze statue of Bogert atop his trusty steed commands the front lawn at city hall.

Because of its large size and location in the desert near the army's tank training grounds, the El Mirador was transmogrified into Torney General Hospital from 1942 to 1945. Then, for seven years after the war, it sat fading and forlorn until investors, led by oilman Ray Ryan, bought the hotel in 1952. They hired celebrity architect Paul R. Williams to refresh the tired dowager. Williams had recently performed similar cosmetic surgery on the Beverly Hills Hotel, adding a pink Late Moderne veneer and jaunty typeface to its façade. The El Mirador enjoyed fifteen dignified years before becoming a Hilton property in 1969 and closing for good in 1973. It subsequently disappeared bit by bit as Desert Hospital, its new owner, expanded. Finally, in 1989, the remaining tower and original lobby were destroyed by fire. The existing tower is a reproduction, a pitiful fate for a once proud symbol of Palm Springs.

LEFT: The El Mirador under construction in 1927. Apparently, none of these men is the hotel's owner, Prescott T. Stevens. RIGHT: The hotel's setting at the foot of Mount San Jacinto was spectacular.

FACING: University of California coeds getting some sun. ABOVE: A mirage-like outpost in the northwest end of the Sonoran Desert.

Willard
No. 1579

ABOVE: Archery, golf, or tennis anyone? This publicity shot was taken in 1930. RIGHT: A young Errol Flynn and wife Lili Damita, c. 1938, in a photo taken by Frank Bogert, the El Mirador's publicity man at the time.

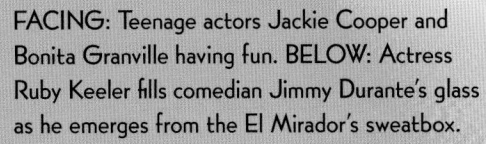

FACING: Teenage actors Jackie Cooper and Bonita Granville having fun. BELOW: Actress Ruby Keeler fills comedian Jimmy Durante's glass as he emerges from the El Mirador's sweatbox.

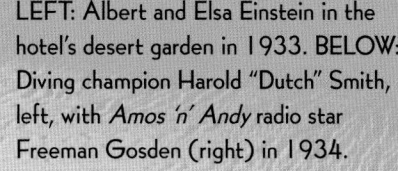

LEFT: Albert and Elsa Einstein in the hotel's desert garden in 1933. BELOW: Diving champion Harold "Dutch" Smith, left, with *Amos 'n' Andy* radio star Freeman Gosden (right) in 1934.

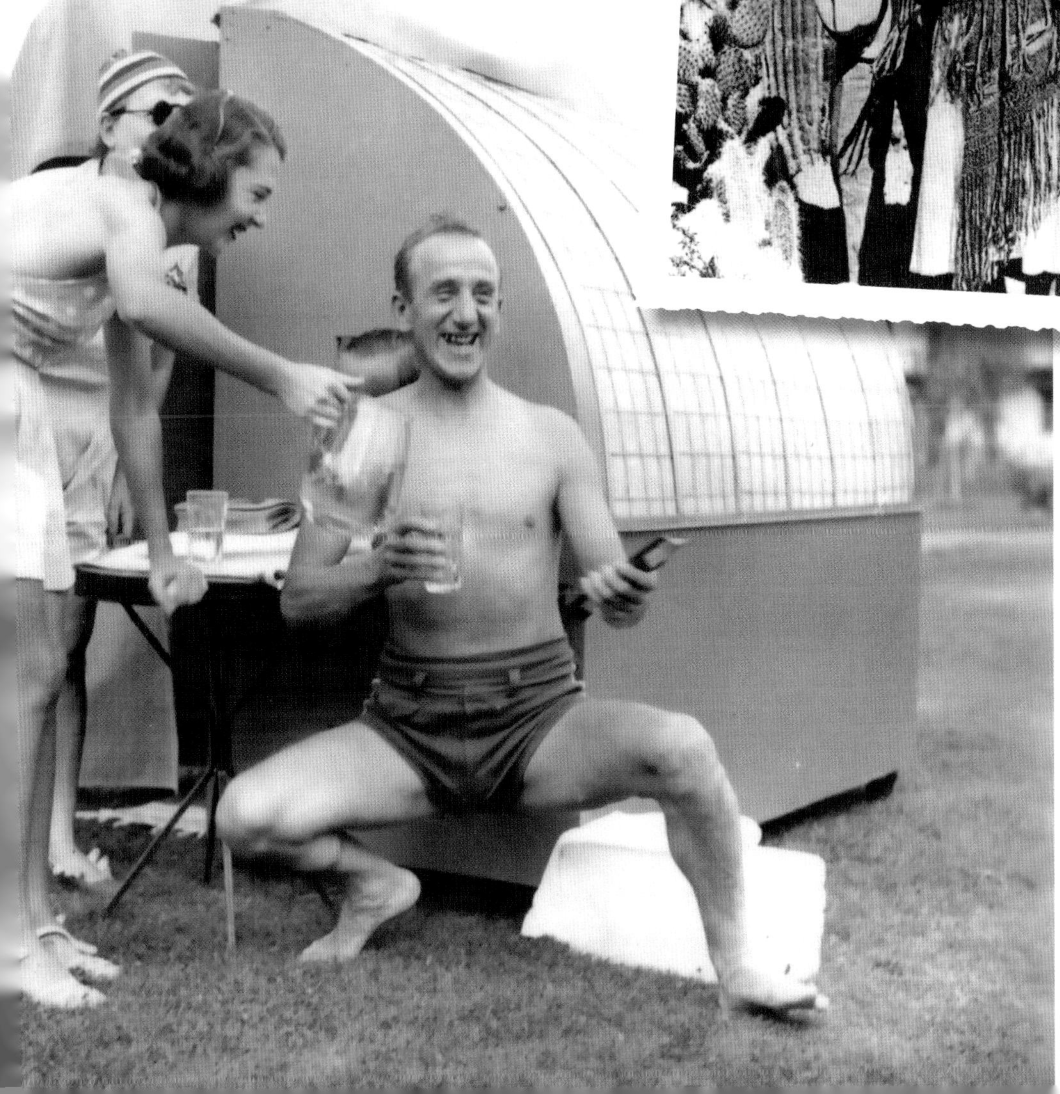

ABOVE: Frank Bogert eyes Annette Powell on the diving board as he emerges from the pool.
RIGHT: Bogert loses his hat riding the hotel's bucking bronco, fully clothed, over the waves in 1937.

LEFT: A cruel Christmas game of "fetch the gift" lures a frightened child to the briny depths. BELOW: Her oblivious mother. RIGHT: *Palm Springs Holiday* cover gal now at the El Mirador.

Presenting the prestigious Schenley Bourbon "Champion" award to Frank Bogert for reasons as yet unexplained.

LEFT: Lounging poolside in 1960, rear cabanas at the ready. INSET: It was all smiles on the outside, but Debbie knew her red lei meant she was on the outs. ABOVE: The last days of the El Mirador. Is that a hearse beneath the porte cochere?

El Mirador Hotel

Architectural Masterworks

Starting in the 1920s, prominent modernists were invited to build in the desert. Rudolph Schindler designed the Popenoe Cabin in 1922; Lloyd Wright the Oasis Hotel, which was completed in 1925; William Gray Purcell—a disciple of Louis Sullivan—his own house in 1933. Albert Frey and Richard Neutra designed modest International style masterpieces: Frey the Kocher-Samson Building in 1934, and Neutra the Grace Miller House in 1937.

In the postwar era, visiting architects who received important Palm Springs commissions included A. Quincy Jones, Paul R. Williams, John Lautner, Rudi Baumfeld of Victor Gruen Associates, William Pereira, Welton Becket, and, again, Neutra and Schindler.

Among the prolific Palm Springs–based architects and designers who demonstrated exceptional talent were Robson Chambers, John Porter Clark, William Cody, Albert Frey, Richard Harrison, Hugh Kaptur, Howard Lapham, Donald Wexler, and E. Stewart Williams. Los Angeles–based William Krisel of the firm Palmer & Krisel designed sleek, modern tract houses for the Alexander Construction Company that would number in the thousands by the mid-1960s. Yet most of the local architects did not consider themselves "Modernists," but rather designers responding to client needs and desert conditions. It just so happened that the functional, elegant buildings they produced would later be categorized as Desert Modern.

LEFT: Architect Donald Wexler and an airport official review plans for the new Palm Springs Airport terminal then under construction in 1965. RIGHT: The dynamic Tramway Gas Station, designed by Albert Frey and Robson Chambers in 1965. Today it's the Palm Springs Visitors Center.

ABOVE: The Oasis Hotel, designed in 1923 by Lloyd Wright. The first truly modern building in Palm Springs. The tower still stands. RIGHT: Bullock's, designed in 1946 by Walter Wurdeman and Welton Becket. FACING: Albert Frey's and A. Lawrence Kocher's 1934 International–style Kocher-Samson Building.

ABOVE: The glamorous Town & Country Restaurant, designed by A. Quincy Jones and Paul R. Williams in 1948.
RIGHT: The Clark & Frey architectural office, designed by John Porter Clark and Albert Frey in 1947.

THE OFFICE OF
HARRY J. WILLIAMS
H. ROGER WILLIAMS
STEWART WILLIAMS
ARCHITECTS

FACING: An early
concept for Palm
Springs City Hall,
unbuilt as depicted.
LEFT: Artist O. E. L.
Graves, left, and
architect E. Stewart
Williams examine
an early model of
the Palm Springs
Aerial Tramway
Mountain Station.

55

ABOVE: Two views of the 1957 Romanoff's on the Rocks restaurant by A. Quincy Jones. It's currently unrecognizable.

FACING: Architect Hugh Kaptur's vibrant rendering of the Steve McQueen house, erected high on Southridge in 1964.

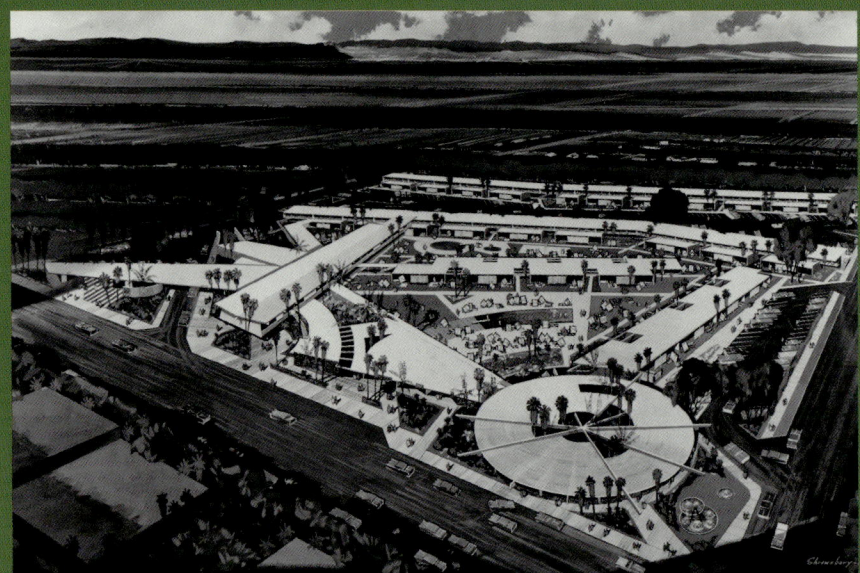

RIGHT: Initial concept for the Agua Caliente Resort Hotel and Spa. The built version was quite different. BELOW: Security First National Bank (now Union Bank), designed in 1959 by architect Joe B. Wong.

Architect E. Stewart Williams, right, at his Santa Fe Federal Savings, designed in 1961. Beautifully restored, it is now the Palm Springs Art Museum Architecture and Design Center, Edwards Harris Pavilion.

LEFT: Rectilinear forms and walls of glass define these Palm Springs Tennis Club condominiums from 1969. ABOVE: Frank Sinatra's 1946 house, which he named Twin Palms, designed by E. Stewart Williams. Sinatra later moved to Rancho Mirage.

LEFT: Architect William Krisel's first Palm Springs project for the Alexander Construction Company—Ocotillo Lodge, designed in 1956. ABOVE: The elegant Chi Chi nightclub in its final space age incarnation by designer Howard Lapham, c. 1960.

FACING: This 1958 Mayfair Market by architect William Cody could pass for a high-Modernist aerospace facility in El Segundo. It was located in the long gone Cameron Center on South Palm Canyon Drive at Mesquite Avenue. BELOW: Cody's Huddle Springs Restaurant, also at Cameron Center, was an organic modern tour de force—a symphony of angles emerging from the desert.

Robinson's department store (Pereira & Luckman, 1958), is a glimmering jewel box of modern design with exterior metal surfaces of anodized gold.

CITY National BANK

CITY National BANK

Inspired by a visit to Le Corbusier's chapel of Notre Dame du Haut in Ronchamp, France, architect Rudi Baumfeld of Victor Gruen Associates paid homage to the master with his design for Palm Springs' City National Bank in 1959. No two sides are alike.

FACING: This monumental statement of financial security by E. Stewart Williams arose in 1960, complete with fountains and reverse arch supports of sturdy concrete. ABOVE: When the E. F. Hutton building talked, people listened. It, like the brokerage firm, has since stopped talking.

ABOVE: The initial attempt to construct John Lautner's Bob Hope house in 1973 did not go as planned. It was rebuilt and commands the crest of Southridge today.

FACING: Agua Caliente tribal chairwoman Eileen Miguel poses proudly in front of the Palm Springs Spa hotel and bathhouse in 1960. It was demolished by the tribe in 2014.

Unique Architecture

Palm Springs is a city of extremes: summer heat, windstorms, towering mountains, proximity to the San Andreas Fault. It also basks in extremes of design. Alien roof forms, absurd door heights, shag carpeting, bad art. Extreme theme architecture has had its day, too. Tiki palaces and Swiss chalets, French châteaus and Neapolitan villas. All flourished side by side with Modernist masterworks. We revel in the contrasts. It's what makes Palm Springs eternally surprising and immensely satisfying.

Greetings from Our Pad!

ABOVE: Putting down roots in the desert. RIGHT: Palm Springs embraced Polynesia in places such as the Tropics Hotel, with its soaring A-framed entrance, rock walls, carved outrigger beams, and, of course, tikis.

FACING: The entrance to the Tropics Hotel's Congo Room, with Sambo's on the right.
Absolutely gorgeous. ABOVE: The Tropics Hotel chain chose Sambo's as their restaurant partner.

A vast tropical paradise in the desert. The Tropics Hotel is just as spectacular today.

The Palm Springs branch of the Don the Beachcomber restaurant chain opened in 1953. Its main entrance was on Via Lola.

In 1960, Aloha Jhoe's moved into William Cody's former Huddle Springs Restaurant at Cameron Center. BELOW: Aloha Jhoe (actually owner Milton F. Kreis of the upscale drugstore chain) gazes proudly at his jaunty sign. John F. DeCuir, set decorator for *The King and I*, designed the interiors and entrance. RIGHT: Aloha Jhoe's mascot was a giant Duk-Duk dancer from Papua New Guinea. Mayor Frank Bogert holds his daughter Donna next to Aloha Jhoe.

Nothing says warm desert weather like an icy mountaintop retreat.

ABOVE: A clean, crisp modern apartment building in Rancho Mirage. FACING: Desi Arnaz built his namesake hotel on the edge of the Indian Wells Golf Club. The Wally Harpst Trio appeared throughout the Coachella Valley, including Aloha Jhoe's.

Banducci's, with its piano bar, was one of the great old-time Palm Springs restaurant and lounge combinations before it closed in 2004. Here, Mama Banducci greets her guests at the outdoor patio.

The Martians have landed . . . in Palm Springs! Apparently, their Regency double-door spacecraft was put up for sale at an unknown location with a 909 street number.

ABOVE: This dazzling modern abode is in the North Shore Estates tract near the Salton Sea. In the 1950s and early 1960s, developers dubbed this enormous inland lake "America's Riviera." FACING: At Bing Crosby's Blue Skies Trailer Village in Rancho Mirage, this owner chose a Mid-century Modern theme. The trailer hitch remained for a quick getaway.

ABOVE: Admiring their 1959 Buick Invicta coupe, which contrasts nicely with the gold-colored walls and planters. Oddly, even the driftwood was painted gold. RIGHT: Walls of glass facing Mount San Jacinto. FACING, TOP: A 1958 Alexander "Swiss Miss"–style residence by Charles Dubois in Vista Las Palmas. FACING, BOTTOM: This swank Movie Colony residence was built in 1961.

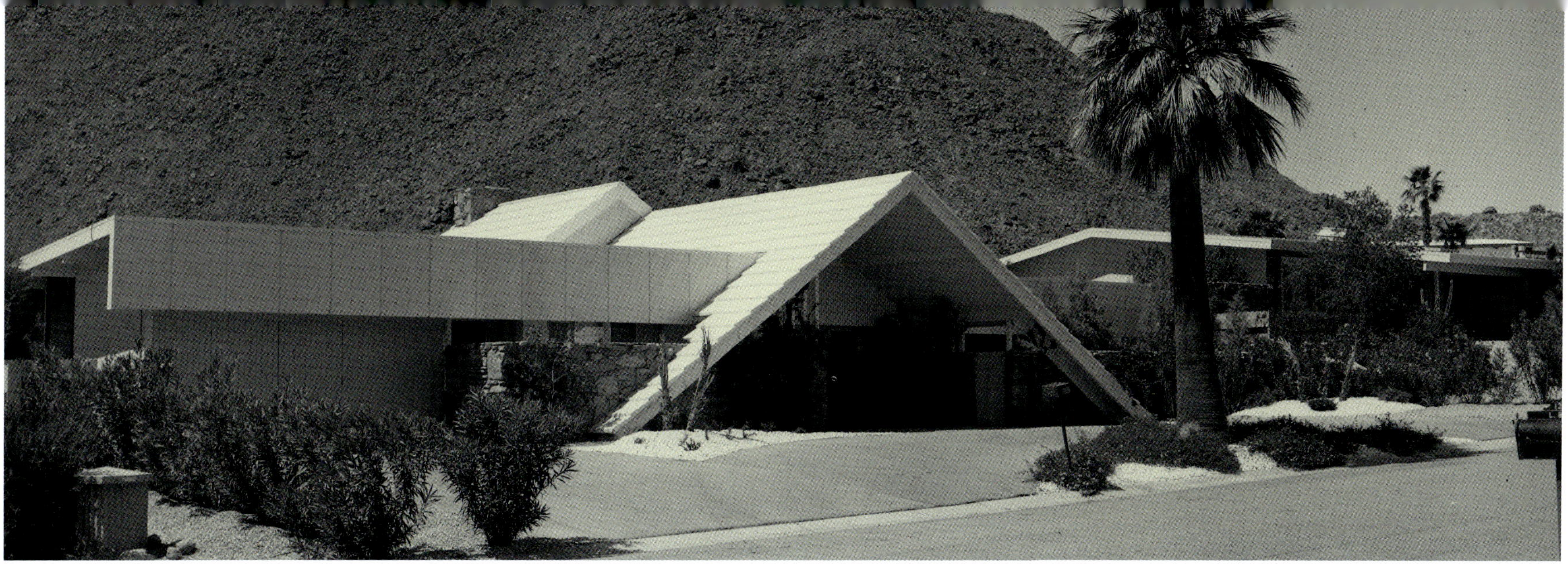

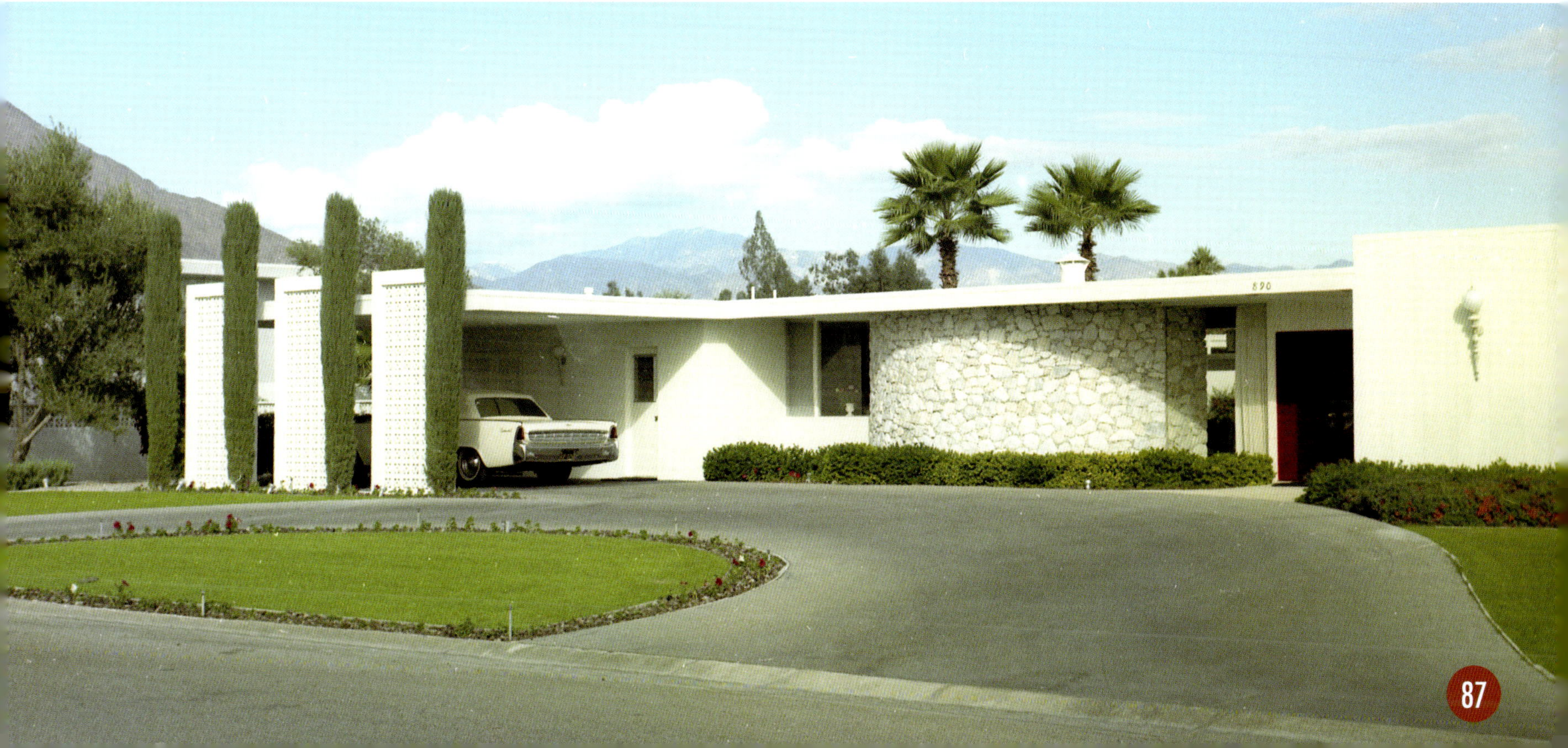
890

FACING: The gorgeous Regency-style entrance of David Hearst Jr.'s residence. But who was the mysterious "W"? ABOVE: Celebrating a time when people weren't afraid of color.

ABOVE: Pierre Paulin's ribbon chairs infuse this room with vitality. FACING: A custom 1960 Vista Las Palmas home inspired by Beverly Hills' deluxe Trousdale Estates. Sliding doors retract into walls for complete indoor-outdoor living. Steps lead from the living room to the pool with cocktails served at the swim-up sunken bar.

ABOVE: Hypnotized by her own artwork, Mrs. Kravitz was unable to move from the corner of the bar.
RIGHT: Bedspreads, bolsters, headboards, and wallpaper merge seamlessly in this elegant boudoir.

LEFT: A bedroom in Elvis's Honeymoon Hideway (originally Robert and Helene Alexander's House of Tomorrow). RIGHT: Perhaps the painting inspired the pink throw pillows and blue bedspread.

Having Fun!

People come to Palm Springs to have a good time, whether for the weekend, season, or in retirement. Swimming, sunning, hiking, golfing, biking, tennis, archery, drinking, dining, dancing, stargazing, sleeping, and fooling around. Chuckwagon breakfasts, horseback riding, piloting a Cessna, shopping at Bullock's or Saks, cruising Palm Canyon Drive in a new Chrysler Imperial, modeling silly Easter hats in Western garb, playing the guitar, joining the Desert Circus Parade. What was once recreational *de rigueur* rapidly becomes *passé*. And vice versa.

ABOVE: Six archers on horseback, one of whom might be Katniss Everdeen. RIGHT: Christmas 1963 with the Squint family.

ABOVE: Casual cowboy. RIGHT: Cocktail hour at the Hotel del Tahquitz, c. 1945. The gal on the left keeps a tight grip on her horse-and-saddle barstool. FACING: What happened to Lena? Palm Springs' Desert Circus Parade, c. 1949.

The SON OF LENA THE HORNED LIZARD

WILD WEST SHOW RODEO

CALIFORNIA 48
88 D 341

RIKSHA, PALM SPRINGS
ROSE PHOTO

LEFT: Riksha was his name and pulling ladies was his game. ABOVE: Mariachi madness at the Hotel del Tahquitz, c. 1938. FACING: Ringing the bell for an early morning Jack Boyer chuckwagon breakfast, part of the ritual of an idyllic Palm Springs holiday.

ABOVE: One of many roadside fruit and date stands that lined Highway
111 in Indio back in 1965. This one had its own motel of "Just Cottages."
FACING: Still kicking up their heels at the Hotel del Tahquitz.

LEFT: Arlene was proud to be the first woman to wear a pantsuit on a transcontinental flight. RIGHT: Descending to the tarmac at Palm Springs Airport, a lovely stewardess offers a helping hand to Grandma Kravitz.

The Desert Circus

1934–1983

The Desert Circus began in 1934 as a way to raise funds for the church rectory on the Agua Caliente Reservation. It soon became the biggest event of the season. Those caught without Western clothes would be arrested by the "High Sheriff" and levied fines—from $10 to $100—by a judge of the Kangaroo Court, with the money going to the church. Fifty years later, the Western theme had lost its cachet and the Desert Circus finally bit the dust. FACING: Desert Circus, 1966. Today, these shirtless guys would be pulling a float of, well, shirtless guys.

ABOVE: The colorful Shriners band marches up Palm Canyon Drive in 1963. It was quite a fez fest, but what's with the yellow socks? FACING, LEFT: Baubles, bangles, and beads on this lavender Nudie Cohn look-alike from 1963. FACING, RIGHT: Another lovely entry in that year's Desert Circus Parade.

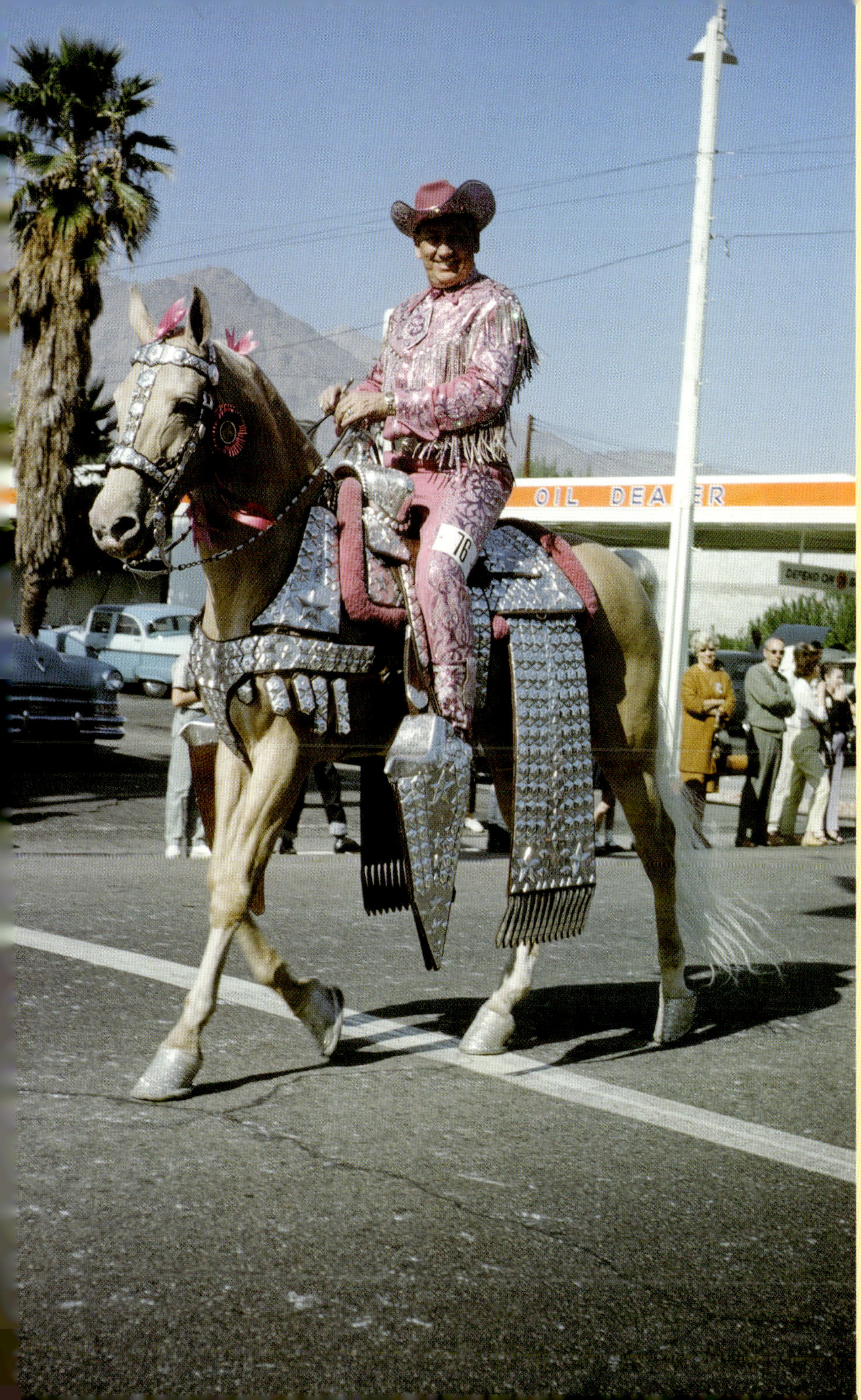
OIL DEA ER
76

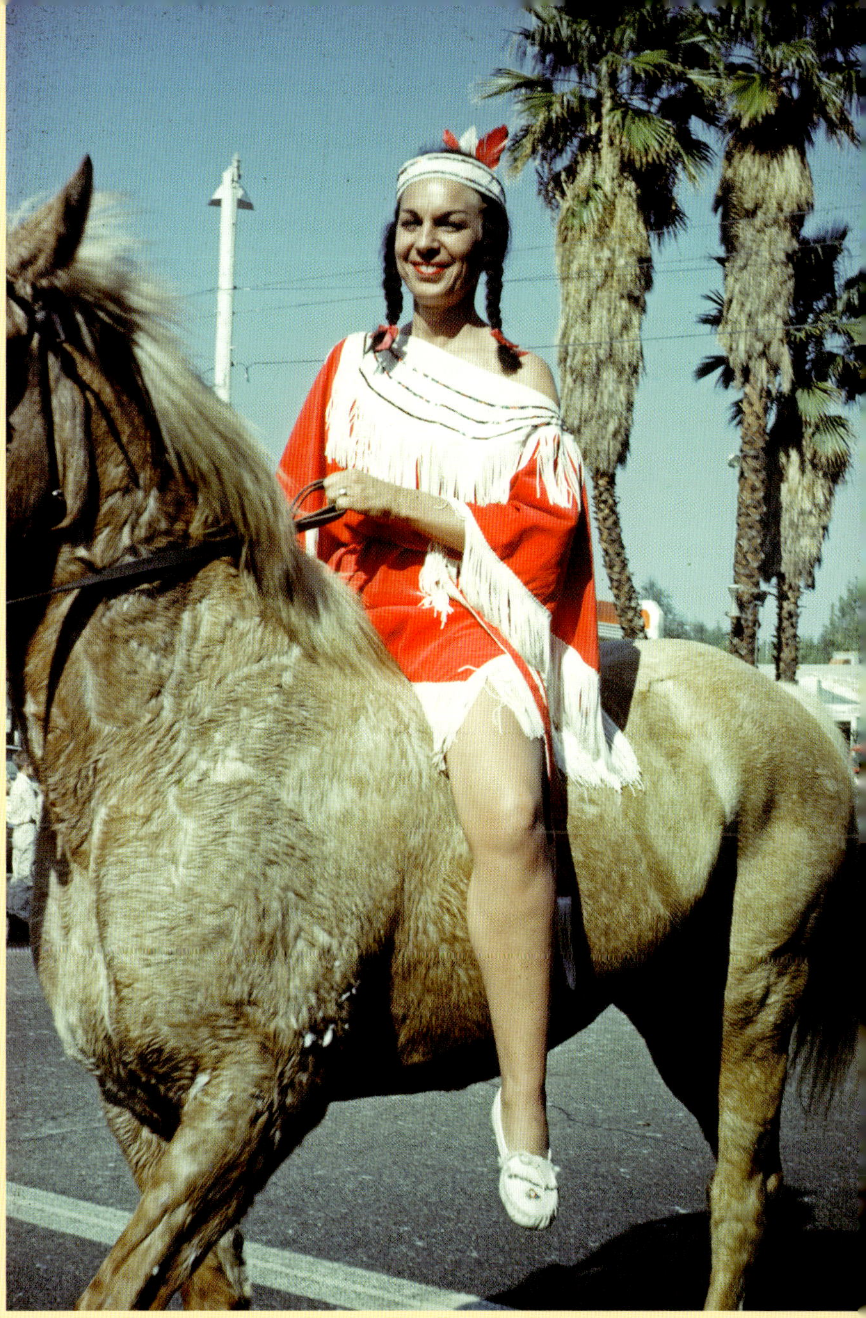

LEFT: Now that her body was tanned all over, Billie was trying to tan her teeth. ABOVE: Goofing with the Guadalajara Trio at The Doll House.

FACING: Looks like he scored a prime parking spot for his 1960 Imperial in front of the glamorous Saks Fifth Avenue on South Palm Canyon Drive. ABOVE: A young couple receives a warm welcome after navigating their 1950 Pontiac convertible and streamlined trailer to the Palm Springs Chamber of Commerce.

ABOVE: Palm Springs pioneer Cornelia White with Winfield Line amongst a field of sand verbena, c. 1953. According to Frank Bogert, Miss White's daily uniform for forty-five years was riding pants, leather puttees, a flowing tie, and an African pith helmet. FACING: Kibitzing at Casitas del Monte. Go U.S.A.!

The Palm Springs Easter Hat Parade

ABOVE: Three male contestants vying for "top" honors. RIGHT: The woman on the right sports a mini head and hat atop her own head and hat. FACING: Marge Riley was the queen of Western wear with her well-stocked store.

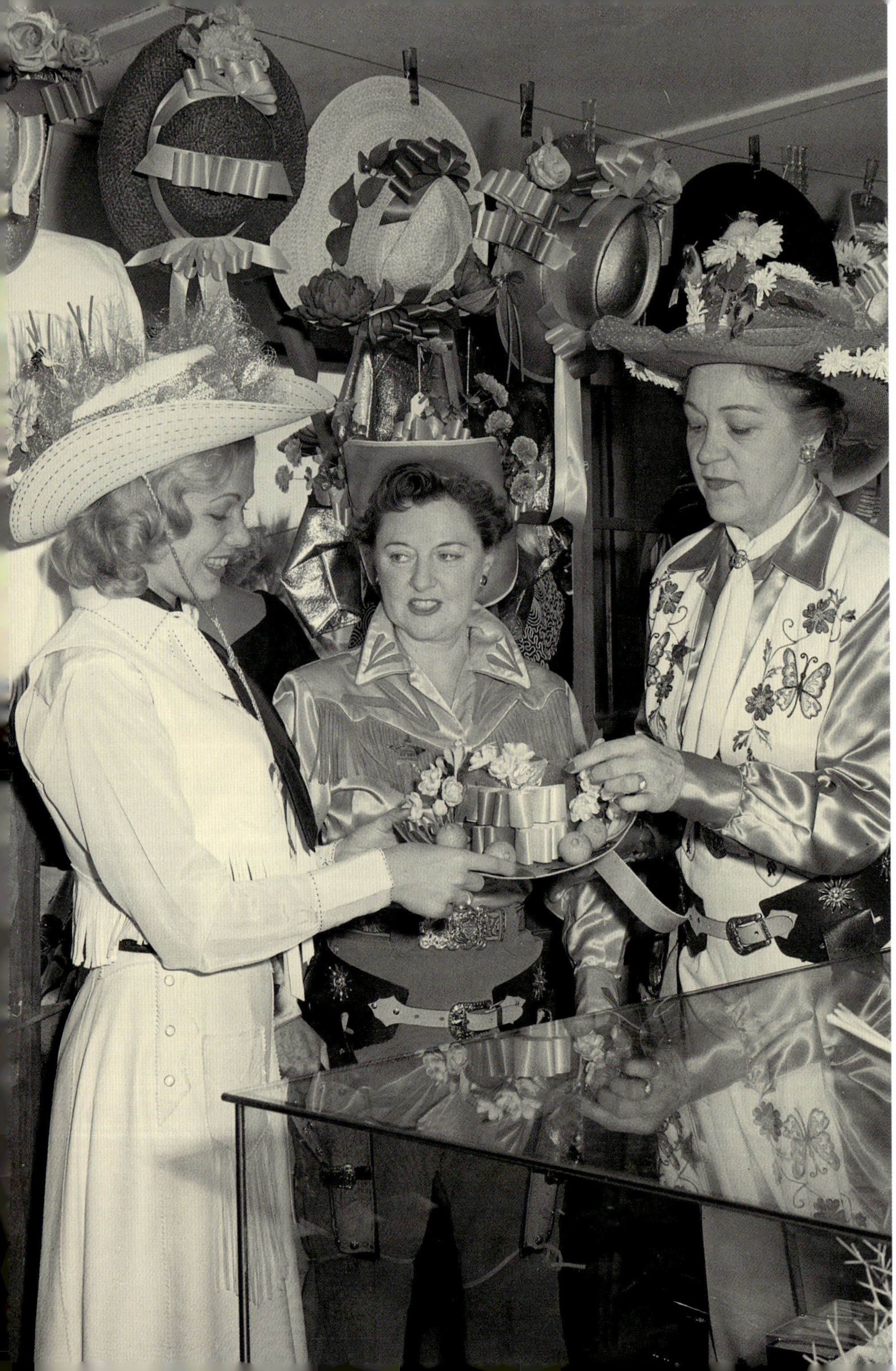

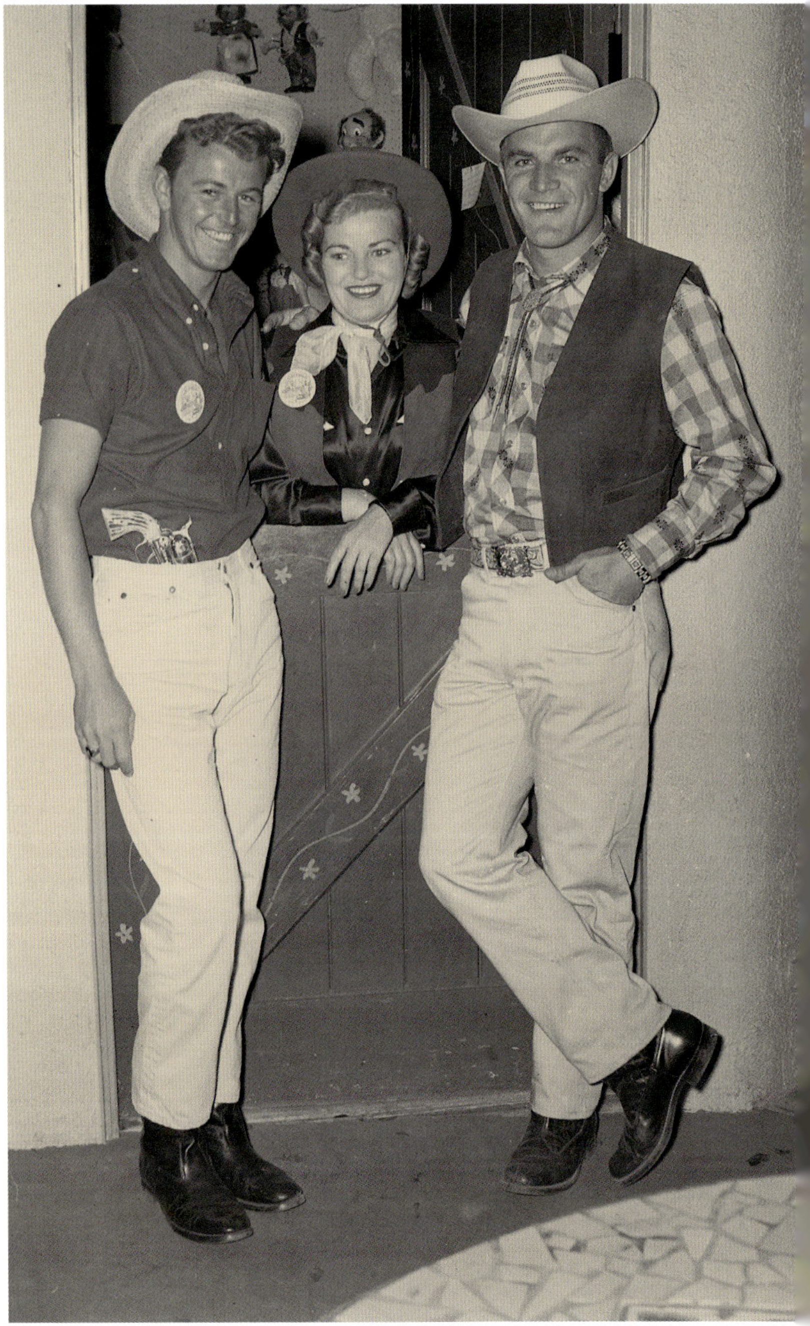

FACING, LEFT: Marge knows a thing or two about hats, as demonstrated here. FACING, RIGHT; LEFT: A gaggle of cowpokes—and an out-of-place cowgirl—showing off their snazzy duds. ABOVE: For the 1958 Texas-themed Desert Circus, songwriter Jimmy Van Heusen (right), Sammy Cahn, and El Mirador owner Ray Ryan (left) cowrote "It's 1200 Miles from Palm Springs to Texas." It was recorded that year by Dean Martin.

BELOW: Voguing at the chic Villa Roma condominiums (left; center) and at the Palm Springs Spa colonnade (right). FACING: It was all anticipation as the gals waited to see who would be selected to pose nude for the portrait session.

Being a Palm Springs model meant sashaying at the airport (left), or a road race photo op poolside at the Biltmore (below; facing).

LEFT: A rare color photo of the man who represents everything that the author aspires to upon retirement in this desert paradise. RIGHT: Phil and Dorothy Boyd at the Living Desert in 1973. BELOW: At The Doll House with, from the left, Frances Bunker, Zaddie Bunker, Dr. Grace Line, and friend in 1961.

LEFT: A spotless '65 Imperial deposits Zaddie Bunker (left) and Dr. Grace Line on Tramway Road. BELOW: Members of the Squint family with Santa Claus in their 1963 Ford Galaxie convertible.

Palm Springs Crazy!

Eccentric. Unconventional. Irreverent. Outrageous. Absurd. Outlandish. Unexpected. Flying grandmas, ridiculous real estate schemes, bad ties, too many liquor bottles on the booze cart. Palm Springs can be pretty darn crazy.

LEFT: Since 1957, KDES (K Desert) has been playing the hits, now at 98.5 FM in Palm Springs. RIGHT: Hand on hip, Mrs. Kravitz imitates the bent arm of the Palm Springs Spa sculpture (left) in 1961.

THE BLACK TENT - DATES,
PALM SPRINGS, CALIF.

ABOVE: Desert nomads erected their Black Tent date stand at the bend where South Palm Canyon Drive turns east. FACING: About every ten years a freak snowstorm or disastrous flood would pass through the village.

ABOVE: The Rogers Stables stagecoach greets American Airlines' *Flagship Palm Springs,* which inaugurated its DC-3 service to the village in 1941. FACING: A caravan of 1963 Thunderbirds and their skirted drivers arrive for the Palm Springs Golf Classic.

In 1951, at age 65, Palm Springs pioneer Zaddie Bunker (see pages 12, 20, 125, 127) earned her pilot's license and became known as the "flying great-grandmother." Her single-engine airplane (left) was named "Zaddie's Rockin' Chair II." Following rigorous Air Force pilot training, she broke the sound barrier in a F-100 Super Sabre jet fighter in 1959. She later applied for astronaut training but was turned down.

ABOVE: Zaddie and jet pilot J. H. Schoca smooch for the cameras beside "Zaddie's Rockin' Chair IV." RIGHT: Zaddie was honored in the 1966 Desert Circus Parade for her aeronautical exploits.

GREAT
RANOMA

Santa Fe Federal Savings

Mrs. Kravitz, another elderly pilot, color
matches her eye with her airplane.

LEFT: Diminutive men's stylist C'Espino was a lonely man who took great comfort in the neckwear that surrounded him. ABOVE: Radiant real estate empress Theresa Press in a carefree moment.

LEFT: The Cork 'n' Bottle's Mrs. Kravitz cheerfully takes a hammer to striking restaurant workers. ABOVE: George Cameron (right) of Cameron Center dedicates his parking lot to our convenience. RIGHT: These trees don't plant themselves, you know.

PREVIOUS OVERLEAF, LEFT: Indio's Empire Polo
Club, c. 1960, now the site of the Coachella Valley Music
and Arts Festival. PREVIOUS OVERLEAF, RIGHT:
Deflowering the virgin desert. BELOW: Nine holes in
Desert Hot Springs. RIGHT: Mr. Kravitz's idea of installing
jet engines to speed up the game was not thought through.

The Riverside County Fair & National Date Festival's Queen Scheherazade and her "harem beauties" aboard a 1959 Imperial. The festival, with its Arabian Nights theme, began in the early 1920s as a celebration of the annual date harvest.

ABOVE: Sniff's display of award-winning dates, pink palms, and a carpet-flying sultan takes center stage in the date festival's exhibition hall. FACING: Mr. Kravitz, sultan of the festival, ignores his harem while inspecting a snazzy 1962 Dodge Polara.

LEFT: Billboards promoting two new developments: The Desi Arnaz Western Hills Lodge (top) and Palm Springs Panorama (bottom) in Cathedral City. ABOVE: This totem pole continues to mark Victoria Park at Via Miraleste and Racquet Club Road. FACING: It's 9,252 cable car miles to the Philippines from the Upper Tram Station, but it's only 2,834 miles to Pittsburgh.

LEFT: Erecting Brontosaurus "Dinny," one of two Cabazon Dinosaurs by sculptor Claude Bell. His belly "hosts an awesome store with something for everyone." RIGHT: A sandstorm in 1975 shut down Interstate 10, stranding cars and trailers.

Celebrities

One of the first celebrities to visit Palm Springs was naturalist John Muir in 1905. However, it was not until Nellie Coffman excised the word "Sanatorium" from "The Desert Inn Hotel and Sanatorium" around 1915 that the rich and famous began arriving in earnest. The flourishing motion picture industry in Los Angeles spawned silent picture stars eager to escape to a convenient desert hideaway. Rudolph Valentino was one of the earliest such guests. In the '30s, the dimpled imp Shirley Temple frolicked at the Desert Inn.

The fabulous El Mirador was the major competition to the Desert Inn in the 1930s, garnering the majority of Hollywood celebrities who preferred it to Nellie Coffman's reserved atmosphere more conducive to eastern and midwestern industrialists. But for sheer decadence, nothing matched the new Racquet Club, opened in 1934 by Hollywood raconteurs Ralph Bellamy and Charlie Farrell. Initially there weren't even accommodations, only a few tennis courts, a restaurant, and a cocktail lounge. But the major draw was the big Racquet Club swimming pool, around which eager starlets would glide, mingling with Hollywood producers and industry hotshots. To confirm the oft-repeated rumor, talent agent Johnny Hyde *did* spot Marilyn Monroe poolside at the Racquet Club in 1947. He would help guide Marilyn's early film career and negotiate her signing of a seven-year contract with 20th Century Fox in 1950.

Celebrities loved Palm Springs because it offered a convenient escape from clamoring photographers and newspaper gossips. Behind the private walls of homes, bungalows, or hotels—and even in Palm Springs restaurants and nightclubs—stars could be more relaxed and uninhibited. Only later, when stars began jetting to private resorts and hideaways, did Palm Springs lose its Hollywood glamour, waiting to be rediscovered by beautiful people in the new century.

LEFT: 1930s Hollywood sex symbol Clara Bow, the "It Girl," gazes longingly at a swarthy Frank Bogert.
RIGHT: Walt Disney, thinking of the future, trains his young followers to protect his cryogenically frozen head.

Palm Springs Home of LUCILLE BALL

LEFT: Golfing buddies Etta Lee and Lucille Ball. ABOVE: Lucy's Thunderbird Country Club house in Rancho Mirage.

BELOW: Palm Springs mayor Florian Boyd with Lucy, Frank Bogert, and Desi Arnaz in 1955. RIGHT: Desi works his bongo drum at the El Mirador's Safari Room.

Palm Springs Home of LIBERACE

Liberace was a Palm Springs regular starting in the 1950s. Here he is relaxing in the kitchen of his first house with agent Seymour Heller (facing, top). Liberace's second Palm Springs abode (facing, below), was a Hollywood Regency tour de force. Here, Cowboy Lee and brother George ride their glittery float in the 1957 Desert Circus Parade. Notice the candelabras on Liberace's white boots.

Palm Springs Music

Liberace

LEFT: A dapper Jerry Lewis, Chi Chi menu in hand, playfully greets an equally dapper Irwin Schuman, owner of the nightclub. ABOVE: Norman Taurog, director of *Palm Springs Weekend* and eight Jerry Lewis movies, has had quite enough of the comedian at Normandy Village. FACING: Marilyn Monroe, who was discovered poolside at the Racquet Club in 1947, revisits its famous Bamboo Room in 1954. On her right with glasses is Joe Kennedy, the future president's father; actor William Powell is to her left.

The Bob Hope Desert Classic began in 1960 and was played at Thunderbird, Tamarisk, Indian Wells, and Bermuda Dunes country clubs. LEFT: Bob Hope and Barbara Eden in Bob's custom "Classic Kart." BELOW: Suntanned volunteers at the 1964 tournament. FACING, LEFT: Comedian Jackie Gleason camps it up. FACING, RIGHT: Caddy Phyllis Diller equipped with weather vane, communication center, dispensary, coffee, snack bar, pencil sharpener, score card adjuster . . .

FACING: The glamorous Gabors: Zsa Zsa, momma Jolie, Eva, and Magda. RIGHT: Newlyweds Natalie Wood and Robert Wagner in 1957.

Every president since Herbert Hoover has spent time in Palm Springs. ABOVE: Mayor Frank Bogert greets President Kennedy in 1962. FACING: Dwight Eisenhower and Kennedy at Ike's Eldorado Country Club residence during the same trip.

The Rat Pack

The Rat Pack and their pals—and sometimes gals—played hard in the desert. Most had houses here. They golfed, boozed it up, cracked wise. They performed for charity events and in local nightclubs and bars. Frank, Dino, Sammy, Jilly, Buddy, Jimmy, Chuck, Bob, Jackie. In the '60s and '70s, they kept Palm Springs famous beyond its expiration date.

Restaurateur "Prince" Mike Romanoff takes a break from his croquet game as Frank Sinatra promotes the annual Palm Springs Police Show charity fundraiser to be held at Palm Springs High School. FACING: Sinatra performs with Les Brown's Band of Renown at the Police Show.

EDDIE ROBERTA GARY
CANTOR LINN CROSBY
PHIL BOB SINATRA
HARRIS HOPE JOAN
DESI DAVI
GINNY ARNAZ
SIMS PALM SPRIN

POLICE
SHOW
DANCE 4,000 SEATS

LES BROWN BAND of RENOWN
SAT. MAR. 24
HIGH SCHOOL PAVILION

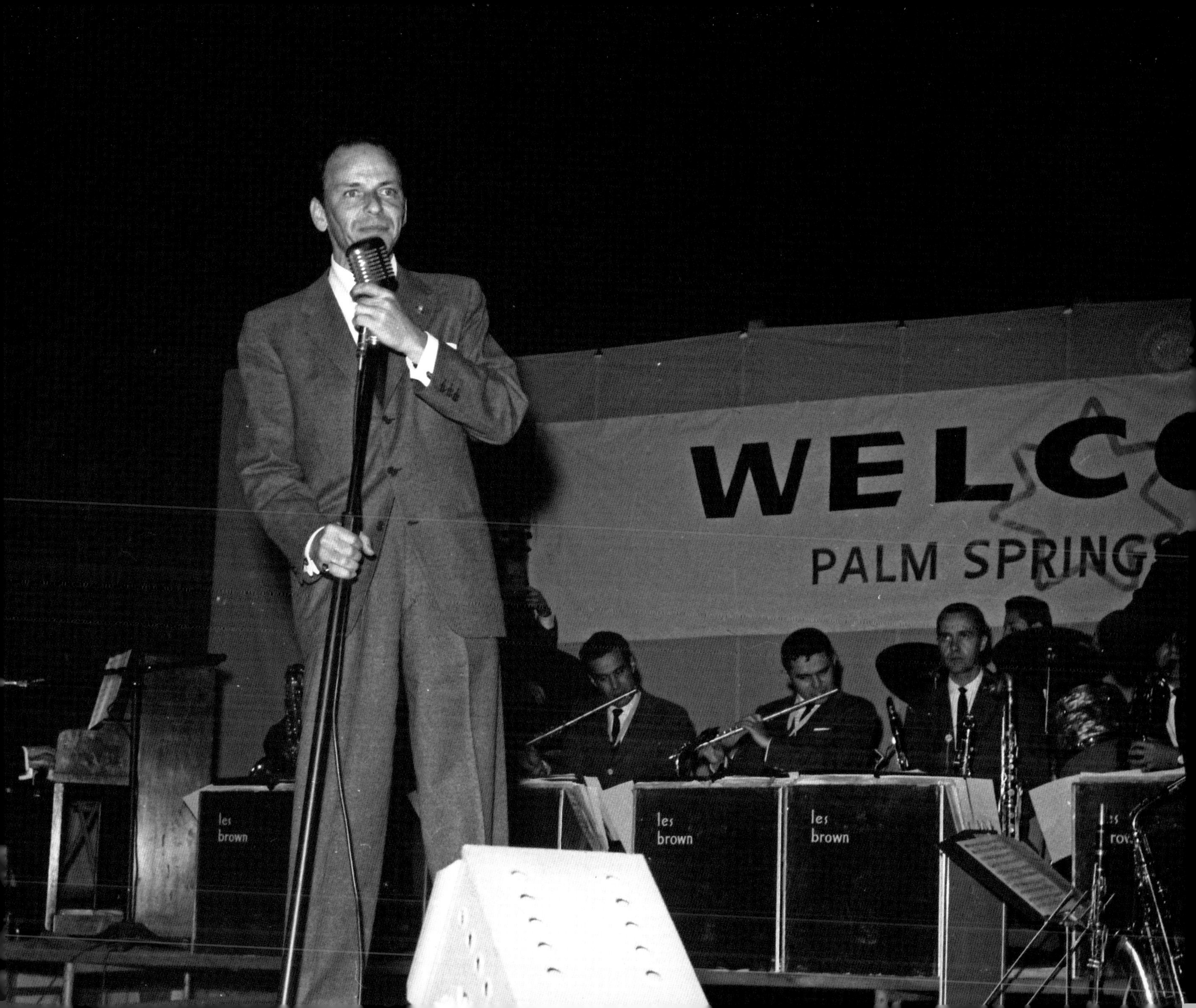
WELC
PALM SPRING
les
brown
les
brown
les
brown

Backstage at the Palm Springs Police Show. ABOVE: Sinatra snogs a member of Palm Springs' finest. RIGHT: Sinatra flanked by songwriter Jimmy Van Heusen, chanteuse Peggy Lee, and oilman, gambler, developer, and El Mirador owner Ray Ryan. In 1977, Ryan was blown up by a car bomb in his native Indiana. FACING: A subsequent Police Show featured Harpo Marx, Jayne Mansfield, Sinatra, and Red Skelton.

Chi-Chi   PALM SPRINGS

Mr _Frank Sinatra_

The Rat Pack were avid golfers. LEFT: Dean Martin takes a swing at the Thunderbird Country Club. BELOW: Sinatra and Sammy Davis Jr. at Tamarisk. FACING: A tight squeeze with Frank, Bob, and Dean at the Bob Hope Desert Classic.

Famous for starring as a widowed western rancher in TV's *The Rifleman,* actor Chuck Connors hosted an annual invitational golf tournament to benefit Angel View Crippled Children's Foundation. The 1970 event at Palm Springs' Canyon Country Club featured Dean Martin (below) and nightclub singer/pianist Buddy Greco (right).

Dino,
after learning
Jerry Lewis was
doing the
catering.

ABOVE: Frank seen here ordering his golf ball into the hole. FACING: Sammy visits Dino in his dressing room at Palm Springs' Riviera Hotel.

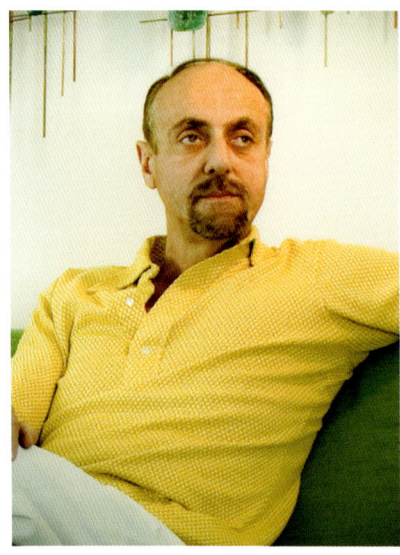

Acknowledgments

Historian Peter Moruzzi has been infatuated with Palm Springs and the Coachella Valley since his first visit in 1990. A few years later, he and his partner bought an unmodified Mid-century Modern house destined to be their retirement home. Born in Concord, Massachusetts, and raised in Hawaii, Moruzzi graduated from the University of California at Berkeley and later attended the American Film Institute in Los Angeles. In 1999, he founded the Palm Springs Modern Committee (PS ModCom), an architectural preservation group. Moruzzi is the author of *Havana Before Castro: When Cuba Was a Tropical Playground, Palm Springs Holiday: A Vintage Tour from Palm Springs to the Salton Sea,* and *Classic Dining: Discovering America's Finest Mid-Century Restaurants.*

To the many generous individuals who assisted in the realization of this book I offer my deepest gratitude, particularly the enthusiastic staff of the Palm Springs Historical Society—Jeri Vogelsang, Renee Brown, and Nicolette Wenzell—who dug deep into the organization's photographic archives to retrieve long-hidden gems. Thanks to Sven Kirsten, Chris Nichols, Lauren LeBaron, and Chris Menrad for their sage advice in image selection, and to Tracy Conrad, Tayva Martinez, Charles Phoenix, James Schnepf, Al Scott, and the Palm Springs Art Museum for sharing photographs from their private collections. For writing several hilarious captions, a tip o' the hat to Courtney Newman. Finally, profound thanks go to my thoughtful and dedicated editor Bob Cooper, to the ultra-talented artist and book designer Kurt Wahlner, and to my publisher and friend Gibbs Smith for the encouragement to create a new book to complement *Palm Springs Holiday.*